SECRET

OF

INTERCESSION

ANDREW
MURRAY

 Whitaker House

All Scripture quotations are from the *King James Version* (KJV) of the Bible.

THE SECRET OF INTERCESSION

ISBN: 0-88368-289-3
Printed in the United States of America
Copyright © 1995 by Whitaker House

Whitaker House
580 Pittsburgh Street
Springdale, PA 15144

1 2 3 4 5 6 7 8 9 10 11 / 05 04 03 02 01 00 99 98 97 96 95

INTRODUCTION

This little book has been prepared with the view of rousing Christians to some right sense of the solemn duty, of the high privilege, and of the wonderful power of intercession. It seeks to point out what a place intercession has in God's plan for the extension of His kingdom, and for the strengthening of the life of His children so that they may receive from Him the heavenly blessings He has to bestow and then go forth to impart them to the world around.

The Dutch original has been found helpful in encouraging Christians to realize their high calling and in helping them to take their place among the Lord's remembrancers who call upon Him day and night. This translation is issued with the hope and prayer that it may be used in Bible classes and prayer meetings to foster that spirit of devotion and prayer which is so essential to the Christian life.

ANDREW MURRAY

Day 1

Intercession

...pray one for another...
—James 5:16

W hat a mystery of glory there is in prayer! On the one hand we see God in His holiness, love, and power waiting and longing to bless man. On the other hand there is sinful man, a worm of the dust, bringing down from God by prayer the very life and love of heaven to dwell in his heart.

But the glory of intercession is so much greater—when a man is bold and asks from God what he desires for others. He seeks to bring down on one soul, or it may be on hundreds and thousands, the power of the eternal life with all its blessings.

Intercession! Would one not say that this is the very holiest exercise of our boldness as God's children? It is the highest privilege and enjoyment connected to our communion with God. It is the power of being used by God as instruments for His great work of making men His habitation and showing forth His glory.

Would one not think that the church would count intercession as one of the chief means of grace? The church should seek above everything to cultivate in God's children the power of an unceasing prayerfulness on behalf of the perishing world.

One would expect believers, who have to some extent been brought into the secret, to feel what strength there is in unity and what assurance there is that God will certainly avenge His own elect who cry day and night to Him. It is when Christians cease from looking for help in external union and aim at all being bound together to the throne of God by an unceasing devotion to Jesus Christ, and an unceasing continuance in supplication for the power of God's Spirit, that the church will put on her beautiful garments and put on her strength, too, and overcome the world.

Our gracious Father, hear our prayer and teach Your church, and teach each of us, what is the glory, what is the blessing, what is the all-prevailing power of intercession. Give us, we pray You, the vision of what intercession means to You, as essential for carrying out Your blessed purpose—what it means to ourselves as the exercise of our royal priesthood, and what it will mean to Your church, and to perishing men, in the bringing down of the Spirit in power—for Jesus' sake. Amen.

Day 2

The Opening of the Eyes

And Elisha prayed and said: LORD, open his
eyes, that he may see...Elisha said, LORD, open
the eyes of these men,
that they may see...
—2 Kings 6:17, 20

*H*ow wonderfully the prayer of Elisha for
his servant was answered! The young
man saw the mountain full of chariots
of fire and horsemen about Elisha. The heavenly host had been sent by God to protect His
servant.

A second time Elisha prayed. The Syrian
army had been smitten with blindness and so
led into Samaria. There Elisha prayed for the
opening of their eyes, and lo, they found
themselves hopeless prisoners in the hand of
the enemy.

We wish to use these prayers in the spiritual sphere. First of all, to ask that our eyes
may see the wonderful provision that God has
made for His church in the baptism with the

Holy Spirit. All the powers of the heavenly world are at our disposal in the service of the heavenly kingdom. How little the children of God live in the faith of that heavenly vision—the power of the Holy Spirit, on them, with them, and in them, for their own spiritual life and as their strength joyfully to witness for their Lord and His work!

But we shall find that we need that second prayer too, that God may open the eyes of those of His children who do not as yet see the power which the world and sin have upon His people. They are as of yet unconscious of the feebleness that marks the church, making it impotent to do the work of winning souls for Christ and building up believers for a life of holiness and fruitfulness. Let us pray especially that God may open all eyes to see what the great and fundamental need of the church is, in intercession which brings down His blessing, that the power of the Spirit may be known unceasingly in its divine efficacy and blessing.

Our Father, who is in heaven, You who are so unspeakably willing to give us the Holy Spirit in power, hear our humble prayer. Open our eyes, we pray You, that we may realize fully the low estate of Your church and people, and as fully what treasures of grace and power You are willing to bestow in answer to the fervent prayer of a united church. Amen.

Day 3

Man's Place in God's Plan

The heaven, even the heavens, are the LORD'S:
but the earth hath he given
to the children of men.
—Psalm 115:16

God created heaven as a dwelling for Himself—perfect, glorious, and most holy. The earth He gave to man as his dwelling—everything very good but only as a beginning with the need of being kept and cultivated. The work God had done, man was to continue and perfect.

Think of the iron and the coal hidden away in the earth, of the steam hidden away in the water. It was left to man to discover and to use all of this, as we see in the network of railways that span the world and the steamers that cover the ocean. God had created all to be thus used. He made the discovery and the use dependent on the wisdom and diligence of man. What the earth is today, with its cities and habitations, with its cornfields and orchards, it owes to man. The work God had begun and prepared was by man to be carried out in fulfillment of God's purpose. And so nature teaches us the wonderful partnership to which God calls man for the carrying out of the work of creation to its destined end.

This law holds equally good in the kingdom of grace. In this great redemption God has revealed the power of the heavenly life and the spiritual blessings of which heaven is full. But He has entrusted to His people the work of making these blessings known and making men partakers of them.

What diligence the children of this world show in seeking for the treasures that God has hidden in the earth for their use! Shall not the children of God be equally faithful in seeking for the treasures hidden in heaven, to bring them down in blessing on the world? It is by the unceasing intercession of God's people that His kingdom shall come, and His will shall be done on earth as it is in heaven (Matt. 6:10).

Ever blessed Lord, how wonderful is the place You have given man, in trusting him to continue the work You have begun. We pray You, open our hearts for the great thought that, through the preaching of the gospel, and the work of intercession, Your people are to work out Your purpose. Lord, open our eyes—for Jesus' sake. Amen.

Day 4

Intercession in the Plan of Redemption

O thou that hearest prayer,
unto thee shall all flesh come.
—Psalm 65:2

*W*hen God gave the world into the power of man, made in His own image, who should rule over it as a viceroy under Him, it was His plan that Adam should do nothing except that which was with God and through God. God Himself would do all His work in the world through Adam. Adam was in very deed to be the owner, master, and ruler of the earth. When sin entered the world, Adam's power was proven to be a terrible reality. It was through him that the earth, with the whole race of man, was brought under the curse of sin.

When God made the plan of redemption, His object was to restore man to the place from which he had fallen. God chose His servants of old who, through the power of intercession, could ask what they would and it should be given to them. When Christ became man, it was so that, as man, both on earth and in heaven, He might intercede for man. Before He left the world, He imparted this right of intercession to His disciples, in the sevenfold promise of the Farewell Discourse (John 15-17), that whatever they would ask He would do for them.

God's intense longing to bless seems in some sense to be graciously limited by His dependence on the intercession that rises from the earth. He seeks to rouse the spirit of intercession that He may be able to bestow His blessing on mankind. God regards intercession as the highest expression of His people's readiness to receive and to yield themselves wholly to the working of His almighty power.

Christians need to recognize intercession as their true nobility and their only power with God—the right to claim and expect that God will hear prayer. It is only as God's children begin to see what intercession means in regard to God's kingdom that they will realize how solemn their responsibility is.

Each individual believer will be led to see that God waits for him to take his part. He will feel in very truth that the highest, the most blessed, the mightiest of all human instrumentalities for the fulfillment of the petition "...as in heaven, so in earth" (Luke 11:2), is the intercession that rises day and night. Christian warriors are pleading with God for the power of heaven to be sent down into the hearts of men. Oh that God might burn into our hearts this one thought: Intercession in its omnipotent power is according to His will and is most certainly effectual!

Day 5

God Seeks Intercessors

And he saw that there was no man, and
wondered that there was no intercessor…
—Isaiah 59:16

From the start God had among His people intercessors to whose voice He had listened and given deliverance. Here we read of a time of trouble when He sought for an intercessor but in vain. And He wondered! Think of what that means—the amazement of God that there should be none who loved the people enough or who had sufficient faith in His power to deliver, to intercede on their behalf. If there had been an intercessor He would have given deliverance, without an intercessor His judgments came down (see Isa. 64:7; Ezek. 22:30-31).

Of what infinite importance is the place the intercessor holds in the kingdom of God! Is it not indeed a matter of wonder that God should give men such power? Yet, there are so few who know what it is to take hold of

His strength and pray down His blessing on the world.

Let us try to realize the position. When God had in His Son wrought out the new creation and Christ had taken His place on the throne, the work of the extension of His kingdom was given into the hands of men. He ever lives to pray. Prayer is the highest exercise of His royal prerogative as Priest-King upon the throne. All that Christ was to do in heaven was to be in fellowship with His people on earth. In His divine condescension God has willed that the working of His Spirit shall follow the prayer of His people. He waits for their intercession, showing the preparation of heart, to what extent they are ready to yield to His Spirit's control.

God rules the world and His church through the prayers of His people. That God should have made the extension of His kingdom to such a large extent dependent on the faithfulness of His people in prayer is a stupendous mystery and yet an absolute certainty. God calls for intercessors: in His grace He has made His work dependent on them. He waits for them.

Our Father, open our eyes to see that You do invite Your children to have a part in the extension of Your kingdom by their faithfulness in prayer and intercession. Give us such an insight into the glory of this holy calling that with our whole heart we may yield ourselves to its blessed service. Amen.

Day 6

Christ as Intercessor

Wherefore he is able to save them to the
uttermost that Come unto God by him, seeing
he ever liveth to make intercession for them.
—Hebrews 7:25

When God had said in Isaiah that He wondered that there was no intercessor, there followed the words: "...therefore His arm brought salvation unto Him..." (Isa. 59:16). "The Redeemer shall come to Zion..." (Isa. 59:20). God Himself would provide the true intercessor, in Christ His Son, of whom it had already been said: "...he bare the sin of many, and made intercession for the transgressors" (Isa. 53:12).

In His life on earth Christ began His work as intercessor. Think of the high-priestly prayer on behalf of His disciples and of all who should through them believe in His name. Think of His words to Peter, "I have prayed for thee, that thy faith fail not..." (Luke 22:32)—a proof of how intensely personal His intercession is. And on the cross He spoke as intercessor: "Father, forgive them…" (Luke 23:34).

Now that He is seated at God's right hand, He continues, as our great High Priest, the work of intercession without ceasing. But with this difference, that He gives His people power to take part in it. Seven times in His farewell discourse He repeated the assurance that what they asked He would do.

The power of heaven was to be at their disposal. The grace and power of God waited for man's bidding. Through the leading of the Holy Spirit they would know what the will of God was. They would learn in faith to pray in His name. He would present their petition to the Father, and through His and their united intercession the church would be clothed with the power of the Spirit.

Blessed Redeemer, what wonderful grace that You call us to share in Your intercession! We pray You, arouse in Your redeemed people a consciousness of the glory of this their calling, and of all the rich blessing which Your church in its impotence can, through its intercession in Your name, bring down upon this earth. May Your Holy Spirit work in Your people a deep conviction of the sin of restraining prayer, of the sloth and unbelief and selfishness that is the cause of it, and of Your loving desire to pour out the Spirit of prayer in answer to their petitions—for Your name's sake. Amen.

Day 7

The Intercessors God Seeks

*I have set watchmen upon thy walls,
O Jerusalem, which shall never hold their
peace day nor night: ye that make mention
of the LORD, keep not silence.*
—*Isaiah 62:6*

*W*atchmen are ordinarily placed on the walls of a city to give notice to the rulers of coming danger. God appoints watchmen not only to warn men—often they will not hear—but also to summon Him to come to their aid whenever need or enemy may be threatening. The great mark of the intercessor is that they are not to hold their peace day or night, to take no rest, and to give God no rest, until the deliverance comes. In faith they may count upon the assurance that God will answer their prayer.

It is of this that our Lord Jesus said: "Shall not God avenge His own elect, which cry day and night unto him…" (Luke 18:7). From every land the voice is heard that the church of Christ, under the influence of the power of the world and the earthly mindedness it brings, is losing its influence over its members. There is but little proof of God's presence in the conversion of sinners or the holiness of His people. With the great majority of Christians there is an utter neglect of Christ's call to take a part in the extension of His kingdom. The power of the Holy Spirit is but little experienced.

Amid all the discussions as to what can be done to interest young and old in the study of God's Word or to awaken love for the services of His house, one hears but little of the indispensable necessity of the power of the Holy Spirit in the ministry and the membership of the church. One sees but little sign of the conviction and confession that it is owing to the lack of prayer that the workings of the Spirit are so feeble and that only by united fervent prayer a change can be brought about. If ever there was a time when God's elect should cry day and night to Him, it is now. Will you not, dear reader, offer yourself to God for this blessed work of intercession and learn to count it as the highest privilege of your life to be a channel through whose prayers God's blessing can be brought down to earth?

Ever blessed Father, hear us, we pray You, and do Yourself raise up intercessors, such as You would have. Give us, we ask You, men and women to act as Your remembrancers, taking no rest and giving You no rest, until Your church again becomes a praise in the earth. Blessed Father, let Your Spirit teach us how to pray. Amen.

Day 8

The School of Intercession

*Who in the days of his flesh, when he had
offered up prayers and supplications with
strong crying and tears...and
was heard in that he feared.*
—Hebrews 5:7

*C*hrist, as Head, is Intercessor in heaven;
we, as the members of His body, are
partners with Him on earth. Let no one
imagine that it cost Christ nothing to become
an intercessor. He could not without this be
our example. What do we read of Him?
"...when thou shalt make his soul an offering
for sin, he shall see his seed...He shall see of
the travail of his soul...therefore will I divide
him a portion with the great...because he
hath poured out his soul unto death..." (Isa.
53:10-12). Notice the thrice-repeated expression in regard to the pouring out of His soul.

The pouring out of the soul—that is the
divine meaning of intercession. Nothing less
than this was needed if His sacrifice and

prayer were to have power with God. This giving of Himself over to live and die that He might save the perishing was a revelation of the spirit that has power to prevail with God.

If we as helpers and fellow-laborers with the Lord Jesus are to share His power of intercession, there will need to be with us as well the travail of soul that there was with Him, the giving up of our life and its pleasures for the one supreme work of interceding for our fellowmen. Intercession must not be a passing interest. It must become an ever-growing object of intense desire for which above everything we long and live. It is the life of consecration and self-sacrifice that will indeed give power for intercession (Acts 15:26; 20:24; Phil. 2:17; Rev. 12:11).

The longer we study this blessed truth and think of what it means to exercise this power for the glory of God and the salvation of men, the deeper will become our conviction that it is worth giving up everything to take part with Christ in His work of intercession.

Blessed Lord Jesus, be pleased to teach us how to unite with You in calling upon God for the souls You have bought. Let Your love fill us and

all Your saints, that we may learn to plead for
the power of Your Holy Spirit to be made
known. Amen.

Day 9

The Power in the Name of Jesus

Hitherto have ye asked nothing in My name: ask, and ye shall receive, that your joy may be full. At that day ye shall ask in my name...
— *John 16:24, 26*

During Christ's life upon earth the disciples had known but little of the power of prayer. In Gethsemane, Peter and the others had utterly failed. They had no conception of what it was to ask in the name of Jesus and to receive. The Lord promises them that in that day which was coming they would be able to pray with such a power in His name that they might ask what they would and it should be given to them.

"Hitherto have ye asked nothing in my name: ask, and ye shall receive, that your joy may be full." (John 16:24). "At that day ye shall ask in My name..." (John 16:26). Therefore you shall receive. These two conditions are still found in the church. With the great majority of Christians there is such a lack of knowledge of their oneness with Christ Jesus, and of the Holy Spirit as the Spirit of prayer, that they do not even attempt to claim the wonderful promises Christ here gives. But where God's children know what it is to abide in Christ and in vital union with Him and to yield to the Holy Spirit's teaching, they begin to learn that their intercession avails much. God will give the power of His Spirit in answer to their prayer.

It is faith in the power of Jesus' name, and in our right to use it that will give us the courage to follow on when God invites us to the holy office of intercessor. When our Lord Jesus, in His Farewell Discourse, gave His unlimited prayer promise, He sent the disciples out into the world with this consciousness: "He who sits upon the throne, and who lives in my heart, has promised that what I ask in His name I shall receive. He will do it."

Oh, if Christians but knew what it is to yield themselves wholly and absolutely to Jesus Christ and His service, how their eyes would be opened to see that intense and unceasing prayerfulness is the essential mark of the healthy spiritual life. The power of all-prevailing intercession will indeed be the portion of those who live only in and for their Lord!

Blessed Savior, give us the grace of the Holy Spirit so that we might live in You, and with You, and for You, allow us to boldly look to You for the assurance that our prayers are heard. Amen.

Day 10

Prayer, the Work of the Spirit

...God has sent forth the Spirit of His Son into your hearts, crying, Abba, Father.
—*Galatians 4:6*

We know what "Abba, Father" meant in the mouth of Christ in Gethsemane. It was the entire surrender of Himself to the very death that the holy will of God's love in redemption of sinners might be accomplished. In His prayer He was ready for any sacrifice, even to the yielding of His life. In that prayer we have revealed to us the heart of Him whose place is at the right hand of God, with the wonderful power of intercession that He exercises there and the power to pour down the Holy Spirit.

The Holy Spirit has been bestowed by the Father to breathe the very spirit of His son into our hearts. Our Lord would have us yield ourselves as wholly to God as He did, to pray like Him, that God's will of love should be done on earth at any cost. As God's love is revealed in His desire for the salvation of souls, so also the desire of Jesus was made plain when He gave Himself for them. And He now asks of His people that that same love should fill them too so that they give themselves wholly to the work of intercession and, at any cost, pray down God's love upon the perishing.

And if anyone should think that this is too high and beyond our reach, the Holy Spirit is actually given into our hearts so that we may pray as Jesus did in His power and in His name. It is the man who yields himself wholly to the leading of the Holy Spirit who will feel urged, by the compulsion of a divine love, to the undivided surrender to a life of continual intercession because he knows that it is God who is working in him.

Now we can understand how Christ could give such unlimited promises of answer to prayer to His disciples; they were first going to be filled with the Holy Spirit. Now we understand how God can give such a high place to intercession in the fulfillment of His purpose of redemption. It is the Holy Spirit who breathes God's own desire into us and enables us to intercede for souls.

Abba Father! Oh grant that by Your Holy Spirit there may be maintained in us the unceasing intercession for love for the souls for whom Christ died. Give, Oh give to Your children the vision of the blessedness and the power which come to those who yield themselves to this high calling. Amen.

Day 11

Christ, Our Example in Intercession

...He shall divide the spoil with the strong, because...he bare the sin of many, and made intercession for the transgressors.
—Isaiah 53:12

*H*e made intercession for the transgressors." What did that mean to Him? Think of what it cost Him to pray that prayer effectually. He had to pour out His soul as an offering for sin, and to cry in Gethsemane: "...Father...thy will be done" (Matt. 26:42).

Think what moved Him so to sacrifice Himself to the very uttermost! It was His love for the Father—that His holiness might be manifest. It was also His love for souls—that they might be partakers of His holiness.

Think of the reward He won! As Conqueror of every enemy He is seated at the right hand of God with the power of unlimited and assured intercession. And He would see His seed, a generation of those of the same

34

mind as Himself, whom He could train to share in His great work of intercession.

And what does this mean for us, when we indeed seek to pray for the transgressors? That we too yield ourselves wholly to the glory of the holiness and the love of the Father. Therefore we can also say: Thy will be done, cost what it may that we too sacrifice ourselves, even to pouring out of our souls unto death.

The Lord Jesus has in very deed taken us up into a partnership with Himself in carrying out the great work of intercession. He in heaven and we on earth must be of one mind. We must have only one aim in life. That aim is that we should love the Father and the lost by consecrating our lives to intercession for God's blessing. The burning desire of Father and Son for the salvation of souls must be the burning desire of our hearts too.

What an honor! What a blessedness! And what a power for us to do the work because He lives and by His Spirit He pours forth His love into our hearts!

Everlasting God of love, open our eyes to the vision of the glory of Your Son, as He ever lives to pray. And open our eyes to the glory of that grace which enables us in His likeness also to live that we may pray for the transgressors. Father, for Jesus' sake. Amen.

Day 12

God's Will and Ours

...thy will be done.
—Matthew 26:42

*J*t is the high prerogative of God that everything in heaven and earth is to be done according to His will and as the fulfillment of His desires. When He made man in His image it was, above all, that his desires were to be in perfect accord with the desires of God. This is the high honor of being in the likeness of God. We are to feel and wish just as God. In human flesh man was to be the embodiment and fulfillment of God's desires.

When God created man with the power of willing and choosing what he should be, He limited Himself in the exercise of His will. And when man had fallen and yielded himself to the will of God's enemy, God in His infinite love set about the great work of winning man back to make the desires of God his own. As in God, so in man, desire is the great moving power. And just as man had yielded himself to a life of desire after the things of the earth and the flesh, God had to redeem him and to educate him into a life of harmony with Himself. His one aim was that man's desire should be in perfect accord with His own.

The great step in this direction was when the Son of the Father came into this world to reproduce the divine desires in His human nature and in His prayer to yield Himself up to the perfect fulfillment of all that God wished and willed. The Son, as man, said in agony and blood, "Thy will be done," and made the surrender even to being forsaken by God. He did this so that the power that had deceived man might be conquered and deliverance procured. It was in the wonderful and complete harmony between the Father and the Son when the Son said, "Thy will be done," that the great redemption was accomplished.

And now the great work of appropriating that redemption is this: that believers have to say, first of all for themselves and then in lives devoted to intercession for others: "Thy will be done in earth, as it is in heaven" (Matt. 6:10). As we plead for the church—its ministers and its missionaries, its strong Christians or its young converts—for the unsaved, whether nominally Christian or heathen, we have the privilege of knowing that we are pleading for what God wills, and that through our prayers His will is to be done on earth as in heaven.

Day 13

The Blessedness of a Life of Intercession

*Then hear thou from the heavens
their prayer and their supplication,
and maintain their cause.*
—2 Chronicles 6:35

*W*hat an unspeakable grace to be allowed to deal with God in intercession for the supply of other's needs!

To be able to take part in Christ's great work as Intercessor is such a blessing. It is wonderful to be in close union with Him and to mingle my prayers with His! What an honor to have power with God in heaven over souls and to obtain for them what they do not even know or think!

What a privilege, as a steward of the grace of God, to bring to Him the state of the church or of individual souls, of the ministers of the Word, or of His messengers away in heathendom, and plead on their behalf until He entrusts me with the answer!

What blessedness, in union with other children of God, to strive together in prayer until the victory is gained over difficulties here on earth or over the powers of darkness in high places!

It is indeed worth living for, to know that God will use me as an intercessor to receive and dispense here on earth His heavenly blessing and, above all, the power of His Holy Spirit.

This is in very deed the life of heaven, the life of the Lord Jesus Himself in His self-denying love, taking possession of me and urging me to yield myself wholly to bear the burden of souls before Him and to plead that they may live.

Too long have we thought of prayer simply as a means for the supplying of our need in life and service. May God help us to see what a place intercession takes in His divine counsel and in His work for the kingdom. And may our hearts indeed feel that there is no honor or blessedness on earth at all equal to the unspeakable privilege of waiting upon God and bringing down from heaven and of opening the way on earth for the blessing He delights to give!

Oh my Father, let Your life indeed flow down to this earth, and fill the hearts of Your children! As the Lord Jesus pours out His love in His unceasing intercession in heaven, let it even be so with us also upon earth, a life of overflowing love and never ending intercession. Amen.

Day 14

The Place of Prayer

These all continued with one accord
in prayer and supplication...
—Acts 1:14

The last words which Christ spoke before He left the world give us the four great notes of His church: "...wait for the promise of the Father..." (Acts 1:4). "But ye shall receive power, after that the Holy Ghost is come upon you: and ye shall be witnesses unto me both in Jerusalem...and unto the uttermost part of the earth" (Acts 1:8).

United and unceasing prayer, the power of the Holy Spirit, living witnesses to the living Christ, from Jerusalem to the uttermost part of the earth—such are the marks of the true gospel, of the true ministry, of the true church of the New Testament.

A church of united and unceasing prayerfulness, a ministry filled with the Holy Spirit, the members living witnesses to a living Christ with a message to every creature on

43

earth—such was the church that Christ founded and such the church that went out to conquer the world.

When Christ had ascended to heaven the disciples knew at once what their work was to be: continuing with one accord in prayer and supplication. They were to be bound together by the love and Spirit of Christ into one body. It was this that gave them their wonderful power in heaven with God and upon earth with men.

Their one duty was to wait in united and unceasing prayer for the power of the Holy Spirit as the enduement from on high for their witness to Christ to the ends of the earth. A praying church, a Spirit-filled church, a witnessing church, with all the world as its sphere and aim—such is the church of Jesus Christ.

As long as it maintained this character it had power to conquer. But alas, as it came under the influence of the world, how much it lost of its heavenly, supernatural beauty and strength! How unfaithful in prayer, how feeble the workings of the Spirit, how formal its witness to Christ, and how unfaithful to its worldwide mission!

Blessed Lord Jesus, have mercy upon Your church, and give, we pray You, the Spirit of prayer and supplication as of old, that Your church may prove what power from You rests upon her and her testimony for You, to win the world to Your feet. Amen.

Day 15

Paul as an Intercessor

*...I bow my knees unto the Father...that
he would grant you...to be strengthened
with might by his Spirit...*
—Ephesians 3:14, 16

*W*e think of Paul as the great mission-
ary, the great preacher, the great
writer, the great Apostle "...in labors
more abundant..." (2 Cor. 11:23). We do not
sufficiently think of him as the intercessor
who sought and obtained, by his supplication,
the power that rested upon all his other ac-
tivities and brought down the blessing that
rested on the churches that he served.

We see above what he wrote to the Ephesians. Think of what he said to the Thessalonians: "Night and day praying exceedingly
that we...might perfect that which is lacking
in your faith.... To the end he may establish
your hearts unblameable in holiness..." (1
Thess. 3:10, 13). To the Romans: "...without
ceasing I make mention of you always in my

prayers" (Rom. 1:9). To the Philippians: "Always in every prayer of mine for you all making request with joy" (Phil. 1:4). And to the Colossians: "...we...do not cease to pray for you...I would that ye knew what great conflict I have for you" (Col. 1:9; 2:1).

Day and night he cried to God in his intercession for them, that the light and the power of the Holy Spirit might be in them. As earnestly as he believed in the power of his intercession for them so also did he believe in the blessing that theirs would bring upon him. "Now I beseech you...that ye strive together with me in your prayers to God for me" (Rom. 15:30). "...[God] will yet deliver us; ye also helping together by prayer for us..." (2 Cor. 1:10, 11). "Praying...for me...that I may open my mouth boldly..." (Eph. 6:18, 19). "This shall turn to my salvation through your prayer" (Phil. 1:19).

The whole relationship between pastor and people depends on the united continual prayerfulness. Their whole relationship to each other is a heavenly one, spiritual and divine, and can only be maintained by unceasing prayer. It is when ministers and people waken up to the consciousness that the power and blessing of the Holy Spirit is waiting for their united and unceasing prayer that the church will begin to know something of what apostolic Christianity is.

Ever blessed Father, we do most humbly ask You, restore again graciously to Your church the spirit of supplication and intercession—for Jesus' sake. Amen.

Day 16

Intercession for Laborers

*...The harvest truly is plenteous, but the
labourers are few; pray ye therefore the Lord
of the harvest, that he will send
forth labourers into his harvest.*
—*Matthew 9:37-38*

*T*he disciples understood very little of
what these words meant. Christ gave
them as a seed-thought to be lodged in
their hearts for later use. At Pentecost, as
they saw how many of the new converts were
ready in the power of the Spirit to testify
about Christ, they must have felt how the ten
days of continuous united prayer had brought
this blessing. This was an example of the fruit
of the Spirit's power—laborers in the harvest.

Christ meant to teach us that however
large the field may be and however few the
laborers, prayer is the best, the sure, the only
means for supplying the need.

What we have to understand is that it is
not only in time of need that the prayer must

49

be sent up but that the whole work is to be carried on in the spirit of prayer. This way the prayer for laborers shall be in perfect harmony with the whole of our life and effort.

In the China Inland Mission when the number of missionaries had gone up to two hundred, at a conference held in China they felt so deeply the need for more laborers for the districts that were unprovided for that, after much prayer, they felt at liberty to ask God to give them within a year one hundred additional laborers and ten thousand pounds to meet the expenses. They agreed to continue in prayer day by day throughout the year. At the end of the time the one hundred suitable men and women had been found with eleven thousand pounds.

The churches all complain about the lack of laborers and funds to meet the need of the world, its open fields, and its waiting souls. Does not Christ's voice call us to the united and unceasing prayer of the first disciples? God is faithful, by the power of His Spirit, to supply every need. Let the church take the posture of united prayer and supplication. God hears prayer.

Blessed Lord Jesus, teach Your church what it means to live and labor for You, in the Spirit of unceasing prayerfulness, that our faith may rise to the assurance that You will in very deed, in a way surpassing all expectation, meet the crying need of a dying world. Amen.

Day 17

Intercession for Individual Souls

...Ye shall be gathered one by one,
O ye children of Israel.
—Isaiah 27:12

*I*n our body every member has its appointed place. This is also true in society and in the church. The work must always aim at the welfare and the highest perfection of the whole through the cooperation of every individual member.

In the church the thought is too often found that the salvation of men is the work of the minister, whereas he generally only deals with the crowd and will seldom reach the individual. This is the cause of a twofold evil. The individual believer does not understand that it is necessary for him to testify to those around him—for the nourishment and the strengthening of his own spiritual life and for the ingathering of souls. Unconverted souls suffer unspeakable loss because Christ is not personally brought to them by each believer they meet. The thought of intercession for those around us is all too seldom found. Its restoration to its right place in the Christian life—how much that would mean to the church and its missions!

Oh, when will Christians learn the great truth that what God in heaven desires to do needs prayer on earth as its indispensable condition. It is as we realize this that we shall see that intercession is the chief element in the conversion of souls. All of our efforts are in vain without the power of the Holy Spirit given in answer to prayer. It is when ministers and people unite in a covenant of prayer and testimony that the church will flourish and that every believer will understand the part he has to take.

What can we do to stir up the spirit of intercession? There is a twofold answer. Let every Christian, as he begins to get an insight into the need and the power of intercession, begin by exercising it on behalf of single individuals. Pray for your children, for your relatives and friends, for all with whom God brings you into contact. If you feel that you do not have the power to intercede, let the discovery humble you and drive you to the mercy seat. God wants every redeemed child of His to intercede for the perishing. It is the vital breath of the normal Christian life—the proof that it is born from above.

Then pray intensely and persistently that God may give the power of His Holy Spirit to you and His children around you, that the power of intercession may have the place that God will honor.

Day 18

Intercession for Ministers

And for me...
—*Ephesians 6:19*

...praying also for us...
—*Colossians 4:3*

Finally, brethren, pray for us...
—*2 Thessalonians 3:1*

*T*hese expressions of Paul suggest how strong his conviction must have been that the Christians had power with God and that their prayer would in very deed bring new strength to him in his work. He had such a sense of the actual unity of the body of Christ. He saw unity in the interdependence of each member, even the most honorable, and on the life that flowed through the whole body. This encouraged him to rouse Christians, for their own sakes and for his sake and for the sake of the kingdom of God, with his call: "Continue in prayer, and watch in the same with thanksgiving; withal praying also for us..." (Col. 4:2-3).

The church depends upon the ministry to an extent that we very little realize. The place of the minister is so high, as the steward of the mysteries of God and as the ambassador for God to beseech men in Christ's name to be reconciled to Him, that unfaithfulness or inefficiency must bring a terrible blight on the church that he serves. If Paul, after having preached for twenty years in the power of God, still needed the prayer of the church, how much more does the ministry in our day need it?

The minister needs the prayer of his people. He has a right to it. He is in very truth dependent on it. It is his task to train Christians for their work of intercession on behalf of the church and the world. He must begin with training them to pray for himself. He may have to begin still farther back and learn to pray more for himself and for them. Let all intercessors who are seeking to enter more deeply into their blessed work give a larger place to the ministry, whether of their own church or of other churches.

Let them plead with God for individual men and for special circles. Let them continue in prayer and watch therein, that ministers may be men of power, men of prayer, and men full of the Holy Spirit. Oh friends, pray for the ministry!

Our Father who is in heaven, we humbly pray You to arouse believers to a sense of their calling to pray for the ministers of the gospel in the spirit of faith. Amen.

Day 19

Prayer for All Saints

*...with all prayer and supplication in the
Spirit, and watching thereunto with all
perseverance and supplication
for all saints.
—Ephesians 6:18*

*N*otice how Paul repeats the words in
the intensity of his desire to reach the
hearts of his readers. "With all prayer
and supplication...watching thereunto in all
perseverance and all supplication." It is, "*all*
prayer, *all* perseverance, *all* supplication."
The words claim thought, if they are to meet
with the needed response.

Paul felt so deeply the unity of the body of
Christ, and he was so sure that the unity
could only be realized in the exercise of love
and prayer. Therefore, he pleaded with the
believers at Ephesus unceasingly and fer-
vently to pray for all saints, not only in their
immediate circle, but in all the church of
Christ of whom they might hear. "Unity is

strength." As we exercise this power of intercession with all perseverance, we shall be de-
livered from self with all its feeble prayers and
lifted up to that enlargement of heart in
which the love of Christ can flow freely and
fully through us.

The great lack in true believers is often
that in prayer they are occupied with themselves and with what God must do for them.
Let us realize that we have here a call to every
believer to give himself without ceasing to the
exercise of love and prayer. It is as we forget
ourselves, in the faith that God will take
charge of us, and yield ourselves to the great
and blessed word of calling down the blessing
of God upon our fellow believers that the
whole church will be fitted to do its work in
making Christ known to every creature. This
alone is the healthy and the blessed life of a
child of God who has yielded himself wholly to
Christ Jesus.

Pray for God's children and the church
around you. Pray for all the work in which
they are engaged or ought to be. Pray at all
seasons in the Spirit for all of God's saints.
There is no blessedness greater than that of
abiding communion with God. There is no
way that leads to the enjoyment of this more

surely than the life of intercession for which these words of Paul appeal so pleadingly.

Day 20

Missionary Intercession

And when they had fasted and prayed,
and laid their hands on them,
they sent them away.
—Acts 13:3

*T*he supreme question of foreign missions is how to multiply the number of Christians who will individually and collectively wield this force of intercession for the conversion and transformation of men. Every other consideration and plan is secondary to that of wielding the forces of prayer.

We take for granted that those who love this work, and bear it upon their hearts, will follow the scriptural injunction to pray unceasingly for its triumph. To such, not only the morning watch and the hours of stated devotion, but all times and seasons will witness an attitude of intercession that refuses to let God go until He crowns His workers with victory.

Missions have their root in the love of Christ, as that was proven on the cross and now lives in our heart. As men are so earnest in seeking to carry out God's plans for the natural world, so God's children should be at least as wholehearted in seeking to bring Christ's love to all mankind. Intercession is the chief means appointed by God to bring the great redemption within the reach of all.

Pray for the missionaries, that the Christ-life may be clear and strong. Pray also that they may be men of prayer and filled with love, in whom the power of the spiritual life is made manifest.

Pray for the native Christians, that they may know the glory of the mystery among the heathen so that with Christ in them they will know the hope of glory.

Pray for the baptism classes and all the pupils in schools, that the teaching of God's Word may be in power. Pray specially for the native pastors and evangelists, that the Holy Spirit may fill them to be witnesses for Christ among their fellow-countrymen.

Pray, above all, for the church of Christ, that it may be lifted out of its indifference and that every believer may be brought to understand that the one object of his life is to help to make Christ king on the earth.

Our gracious God, our eyes are on You. Will You not in mercy hear our prayer, and by the Holy Spirit reveal the presence and the power of Christ in the work of Your servants? Amen.

Day 21

The Grace of Intercession

Continue in prayer, and watch in the same with thanksgiving...praying also for us...
—*Colossians 4:2-3*

There is nothing that can bring us nearer to God, and lead us deeper into His love, than the work of intercession. There is nothing that can give us a higher experience of the likeness of God than the power of pouring out our hearts into the bosom of God in prayer for men around us. There is nothing that can so closely link us to Jesus Christ, the great Intercessor, and give us the experience of His power and Spirit resting on us as the yielding of our lives to the work of bringing the great redemption into the hearts and lives of our fellow-men. There is nothing in which we shall know more of the powerful working of the Holy Spirit than the prayer breathed by Him into our hearts, "Abba, Father," in all the fullness of meaning that it had for Christ in Gethsemane. There is nothing that can so help us to prove the power and the faithfulness of God to His Word as when we reach out in intercession to the multitudes either in the church of Christ or in the darkness of heathenism. We pour out our souls as a living sacrifice before God. Our one persistent plea is that He shall, in answer to our prayer, open the windows of heaven and send down His abundant blessing. God will be glorified, our souls will reach their highest destiny, and God's kingdom will come.

There is nothing that will so help us to understand and to experience the living unity of the body of Christ, and the irresistible power that it can exert, as the daily and continued fellowship with God's children. His children stand together in the persistent plea that God will arise and have mercy upon Zion and make her a light and a life to those who are sitting in darkness. Oh my brother, how little we realize what we are losing in not living in fervent intercession! What could we possibly lose for ourselves and for the world if we allow God's Spirit, as a Spirit of grace and of supplication, to master our whole being?

In heaven Christ lives to pray. His whole communion with His Father is prayer—an asking and receiving of the fullness of the Spirit for His people. God delights in nothing so much as in prayer. Shall we not learn to believe that the highest blessings of heaven will be unfolded to us as we pray more?

Blessed Father, pour down the Spirit of supplication and intercession on Your people—for Jesus Christ's sake. Amen.

United Intercession

There is one body, and one Spirit...
—Ephesians 4:4

*O*ur own bodies teach us how essential for their health and strength it is that every member should take its full share in seeking the welfare of the whole. It is even so in the body of Christ. There are, alas, too many who look upon salvation only in connection with their own happiness. There are those, again, who know that they live not unto themselves. They truly seek in prayer and work to bring others to share in their happiness; however, they do not yet understand that in addition to their personal circle or church, they have a calling to enlarge their hearts to take the whole body of Christ Jesus into their love and their intercession.

Yet this is what the Spirit and the love of Christ will enable them to do. It is only when intercession for the whole church, by the whole church, ascends to God's throne that the Spirit of unity and of power can have its full sway. The desire that has been awakened for closer union between the different branches of the church of Christ is cause for thanksgiving. And yet the difficulties are so great and, in the case of different nationalities of the world, so apparently inseperable that the thought of a united church on earth appears beyond reach.

Let us bless God that there is a unity in Christ Jesus that is deeper and stronger than any visible manifestation could make it. There is a way in which even now, amidst all diversity of administrations, the unity can be practically exemplified and utilized as the means of an unthought-of accession of divine strength and blessing in the work of the kingdom. It is in the cultivation and increase of the Spirit and in the exercise of intercession that the true unity can be realized. As believers are taught what is the meaning of their calling as a royal priesthood, they are led to see that God is not confined in His love or promises to their limited spheres of labor. God invites them to enlarge their hearts and like Christ—we may say like Paul too—to pray for all who believe, or can yet be brought to believe, that this earth and the church of Christ in it will, by intercession, be bound to the throne of heaven as it has never yet been.

Let Christians and ministers agree and bind themselves together for this worldwide intercession. It will strengthen the confidence that prayer will be heard and that their prayers too will become indispensable for the coming of the kingdom.

Day 23

Unceasing Intercession

Pray without ceasing.
—1 Thessalonians 5:17

*H*ow different the standard of the average Christian is, with regard to a life in the service of God, from that which Scripture gives us. The average Christian's chief thought is personal safety: grace to pardon our sin and to live such a life as may secure our entrance into heaven. How high above this is the Bible standard—a Christian surrendering himself with all his powers, with his time and thought and love wholly yielded to the glorious God who has redeemed him, whom he now delights in serving, in whose fellowship is heaven begun.

To the average Christian the command "Pray without ceasing" is simply a needless and impossible life of perfection. Who can do it? We can get to heaven without it. To the true believer, on the contrary, it holds out the promise of the highest happiness, of a life crowned by all the blessings that can be brought down on souls through his intercession. And as he perseveres, it becomes increasingly his highest aim upon earth, his highest joy, his highest experience of the wonderful fellowship with the holy God.

"Pray without ceasing!" Let us take that word in a large faith, as a promise of what God's Spirit will work in us, of how close and intimate our union to the Lord Jesus can be, and of our likeness to Him, in His ever-blessed intercession at the right hand of God. Let it become to us one of the chief elements of our heavenly calling to be consciously the stewards and administrators of God's grace to the world around us. As we think of how Christ said, "I in them, and thou in me..." (John 17:23), let us believe that just as the Father worked in Him, so Christ, the interceding High Priest, will work and pray in us. As the faith of our high calling fills our hearts we shall begin literally to feel that there is nothing on earth for one moment to be compared with the privilege of being God's priests. This privilege includes walking without intermission in His holy presence, bringing the burden of the souls around us to the footstool of His throne, and receiving at His hands the power and blessing to dispense to our fellow-men.

This is indeed the fulfillment of the Word of old, which said that man was created in the likeness and the image of God (Gen. 1:27).

Day 24

Intercession, the Link between Heaven and Earth

...Thy will be done, as in heaven, so in earth.
—Luke 11:2

*W*hen God created heaven and earth, He meant heaven to be the divine pattern to which earth was to be conformed; "as in heaven, so on earth" was to be the law of its existence.

This truth calls us to think of what constitutes the glory of heaven. God is all in all there. Everything lives in Him and to His glory. We then think of what this earth has now become with all its sin and misery. Here on earth the great majority of the race is without any knowledge of the true God, and the remainder are nominal Christians who are for the greater part utterly indifferent to His claims and estranged from His holiness and love. What a revolution, what a miracle is needed if the word is to be fulfilled: "As in heaven, so in earth."

How is this word ever to come true? Through the prayers of God's children. Our Lord teaches us to pray for it. Intercession is to be the great link between heaven and earth. The intercession of the Son, begun upon earth, continued in heaven, and carried on by His redeemed people upon earth, will bring about the mighty change: "As in heaven, so in earth." As Christ said, "...I come to do Thy will, O God" (Heb. 10:9), until He prayed the great prayer in Gethsemane, "...Thy will be done" (Matt. 26:42). So His redeemed ones, who yield themselves fully to His mind and Spirit, make His prayer their own and unceasingly send up the cry, "Thy will be done, as in heaven, so in earth."

Every prayer of a parent for a child, of a believer for the saving of the lost, or for more grace to those who have been saved, is part of the great unceasing cry going up day and night from this earth, "As in heaven, so in earth."

But it is when God's children not only learn to pray for their immediate circles and interests but enlarge their hearts to take in the whole church and the whole world, that their united supplication will have power with God. Then the day will be hastened when it shall indeed be "as in heaven so in earth"—the whole earth filled with the glory of God. Child of God, will you not yield yourself, like Christ, to live with this one prayer: "Father...Thy will be done, as in heaven, so in earth"?

"Our Father, which art in heaven, hallowed be Thy name. Thy kingdom come, Thy will be done, as in heaven, so in earth. Amen" *(Luke 11:2).*

Day 25

The Fulfillment of God's Desires

For the LORD hath chosen Zion...
for His habitation...here will I dwell;
for I have desired it.
—Psalm 132:13-14

*H*ere you have the one great desire of God that moved Him in the work of redemption. His heart longed for man to dwell with him and in him.

To Moses He said: "And let them make me a sanctuary; that I may dwell among them" (Exod. 25:8). And just as Israel had to prepare the dwelling for God, even so His children are now called to yield themselves for God to dwell in them and to win others to become His habitation. As the desire of God towards us fills the heart, it will waken within us the desire to gather others around us to become His dwelling too.

What an honor! What a high calling to count my worldly business as entirely secondary and to find my life and my delight in winning souls in whom God may find His heart's delight! "Here will I dwell; for I have desired it."

And this is what I can above all do through intercession. I can pray for God to give His Holy Spirit to those around me. It is God's great plan that man himself shall build Him a habitation. It is in answer to the unceasing intercession of His children that God will give His power and blessing. As this great desire of God fills us, we shall give ourselves wholly to labor for its fulfillment.

Think of David when he thought of God's desire to dwell in Israel, how he said: "I will not give sleep to mine eyes, or slumber to mine eyelids, until I find out a place for the Lord, an habitation for the mighty God of Jacob" (Ps. 132:4-5). And shall we not, to whom it has been revealed what that indwelling of God may be, give our lives for the fulfillment of His heart's desire?

Oh let us begin, as never before, to pray for our children, for the souls around us, and for all the world. And that not only because we love them but because God longs for them and gives us the honor of being the channels through whom His blessing is brought down. Children of God, awake to the realization of what it means that God is seeking to train you as intercessors through whom the great desire of His loving heart can be satisfied!

Oh God, who has said of human hearts, "Here will I dwell, for I have desired it," teach us, we pray You, to pray, day and night, that the desire of Your heart may be fulfilled. Amen.

Day 26

The Fulfillment of Man's Desire

Delight thyself also in the LORD; and he shall give thee the desires of thine heart.
—Psalm 37:4

God is love, an ever-flowing fountain out of which streams the unceasing desire to make His creatures the partakers of all the holiness and the blessedness there is in Himself. This desire for the salvation of souls is in very deed God's perfect will, His highest glory.

This loving desire of God to get His place in the heart of men, He imparts to all His children who are willing to yield themselves wholly to Him. It is in this that the likeness and image of God consist—to have a heart in which His love takes complete possession and leads us to find spontaneously our highest joy in loving as He does.

It is thus that our text finds its fulfillment: "Delight thyself also in the Lord," and in His life of love, "and He shall give thee the desires of thine heart." Count upon it that the intercession of love, rising up to heaven, will be met with the fulfillment of the desire of our heart. We may be sure that, as we delight in what God delights in, such prayer is inspired by God and will have its answer. And our prayer becomes unceasingly, "Your desires, oh my Father, are mine. Your holy will of love is my will too."

In fellowship with Him we get the courage, with our whole will and strength, to bring before His throne the persons or the circles in which we are interested with an ever-growing confidence that our prayer will be heard. As we reach out in yearning love, we shall get the power to take hold of the will of God to bless and to believe that God will work out His own blessed will in giving us the desire of our hearts. He will do this because the fulfillment of His desire has been the delight of our souls.

We then become, in the highest sense of the word, God's fellow-laborers. Our prayer becomes part of God's divine work of reaching and saving the lost. And we learn to find our happiness in losing ourselves in the salvation of those around us.

Our Father, teach us that nothing less than delighting ourselves in You, and in Your desires toward men, can inspire us to pray right, and give us the assurance of an answer. Amen.

Day 27

My Great Desire

*One thing have I desired of the LORD, that will
I seek after; that I may dwell in the house of
the LORD all the days of my life,
to behold the beauty of the LORD,
and to inquire in his temple.*
—*Psalm 27:4*

*H*ere we have man's response to God's
desire to dwell in us. When the desire
of God towards us begins to rule the
life and heart, our desire is fixed on one thing,
and that is, to dwell in the house of the Lord
all the days of our life. Dwelling thus means to
behold the beauty of the Lord, to worship Him
in the beauty of holiness, and then to inquire
in His temple and learn what it means that
God has said: "...I the Lord have spoken it,
and will do it" (Ezek. 22:14) and "...I will yet
for this be inquired of by the house of Israel,
to do it for them..." (Ezek. 36:37).

The more we realize the desire of God's
love to give His rest in the heart, and the

more our desire is thus quickened to dwell every day in His temple and behold His beauty, the more the Spirit of intercession will grow upon us to claim all that God has promised in His new covenant. Whether we think of our church and country, of our home and school, of our nearer or wider circle; whether we think of the saved and all their needs, or the unsaved and their danger, the thought that God is indeed longing to find His home and His rest in the hearts of men, if He be only "inquired of," will rouse our whole being to strive for Zion's sake not to hold our peace. All the thoughts of our feebleness and unworthiness will be swallowed up in the wonderful assurance that He has said of human hearts: "This is my rest for ever; here will I dwell, for I have desired it" (Ps. 132:14).

Our faith begins to sees how high our calling is and how indispensable God has made fervent, intense, persistent prayer as the condition of His purpose being fulfilled. We are then drawn to give up our life to a closer walk with God. We will wait unceasingly upon Him and will become a testimony to our fellow believers of what God will do in them and in us.

Is it not wonderful beyond all thought, this divine partnership in which God commits the fulfillment of His desires to our keeping? Shame on us that we have so little realized it!

Our Father in heaven, we ask You, give, give in power, the Spirit of grace and supplication to Your people—for Jesus' sake. Amen.

Day 28

Intercession Day and Night

And shall not God avenge His own elect, which
cry day and night unto him, though
he bear long with them?
—Luke 18:7

*W*hen Nehemiah heard of the destruction of Jerusalem, he cried to God: "...hear the prayer of thy servant, which I pray before thee now, day and night..." (Neh. 1:6). God said of the watchmen set on the walls of Jerusalem: "...[They] shall never hold their peace day nor night..." (Isa. 62:6). And Paul writes: "Night and day praying exceedingly ...to the end he may establish your hearts unblamable in holiness before God, even our Father" (1 Thess. 3:10, 13).

Is such prayer night and day really needed and really possible? Most assuredly, when the heart is first so entirely possessed by the desire that it cannot rest until this is fulfilled. The life has so come under the power of the heavenly blessing that nothing can keep it from sacrificing all to obtain it.

When a child of God begins to get a real vision into the need of the church and of the world, a vision of the divine redemption which God has promised in the outpouring of His love into our hearts, a vision of the power of true intercession to bring down the heavenly blessing, a vision of the honor of being allowed as intercessors to take part in that work, it comes as a matter of course that he regards the work as the most heavenly thing on earth—as intercessor to cry day and night to God for the revelation of His mighty power.

Let us learn from David, who said: "For the zeal of thine house hath eaten me up..." (Ps. 69:9). Let us learn from Christ our Lord, of whom these words were so intensely true, that there is nothing so much worth living for as this one thought—how to satisfy the heart of God in His longing for human fellowship and affection and how to win hearts to be His dwelling-place. And we also will not give ourselves any rest until we have found a place for the Mighty One in our hearts and yielded ourselves to the great work of intercession for so many after whom the desires of God are going out.

God grant that our hearts may be so brought under the influence of these divine truths that we may in very deed yield ourselves to make our devotion to Christ, and our longing to satisfy the heart of God, the chief object of our life.

Lord Jesus, the great Intercessor, who finds in it all Your glory, breath, we pray You, from Your own Spirit into our hearts—for Your name's sake. Amen.

Day 29

The High Priest and His Intercession

...We have such an High priest...he is able also to save them to the uttermost that come unto God by him, seeing he ever liveth to make intercession for them.
—*Hebrews 8:1; 7:25*

*I*n Israel, what a difference there was between the high priest and the priests and Levites. The high priest alone had access to the Holiest of All. He bore on his forehead the golden crown engraved with "Holiness to the Lord," and by his intercession on the great Day of Atonement, he bore the sins of the people. The priests brought the daily sacrifices and stood before the Lord and came out to bless the people. The difference between high priest and priest was great. But still greater was the unity; the priests formed one body with the high priest, sharing with him the power to appear before God to receive and dispense His blessing to His people.

It is even so with our great High Priest. He alone has power with God, in a never-ceasing intercession, to obtain from the Father what His people need. And yet, infinite though the distance be between Him and the royal priesthood that surrounds Him for His service, the unity and the fellowship into which His people have been taken up with Him is no less infinite than the apparent diversity. The blessing that He obtains from His Father for us, He holds for His people to receive from Him through their fervent supplication, to be dispensed to the souls among whom He has placed them as His witnesses and representatives.

As long as Christians simply think of being saved, and of a life which will make that salvation secure, they never can understand the mystery of the power of intercession to which they are called.

But when once they realize that salvation means a vital life-union with Jesus Christ; an actual sharing of His life dwelling and working in us; and the consecration of our whole being, to live and labor, to think and will, and find our highest joy in living as a royal priesthood; the church will put on her strength and prove, in dealings with God and man, how truly the likeness and the power of Christ dwell in her.

Oh God that you would open our hearts to know and prove what our royal priesthood is—what the real meaning is of our living and praying in the name of Jesus, that what we ask shall indeed be given to us! Oh Lord Jesus, our Holy High Priest, breath the spirit of Your own holy priesthood into our hearts. Amen.

Day 30

A Royal Priesthood

*Call unto Me, and I will answer thee, and
show thee great and mighty things,
which thou knowest not.*
—Jeremiah 33:3

*A*s you plead for the great mercies of the
new covenant to be bestowed, take with
you these thoughts:

(1)The infinite willingness of God to
bless: His very nature is a pledge of it. He delights in mercy. He waits to be gracious. His
promises and the experience of His saints as-
sure us of it.

(2) Why then does the blessing so often
tarry? In creating man with a free will and
making him a partner in the rule of the earth,
God limited Himself. He made Himself dependent on what man would do. Man by his
prayer would hold the measure of what God
could do in blessing.

(3) Think of how God is hindered and dis-
appointed when His children do not pray or

pray but little. The low, feeble life of the church, the lack of the power of the Holy Spirit for conversion and holiness, is all owing to the lack of prayer. How different would be the state of the church and of heathendom if God's people were to take no rest in calling upon Him!

(4) And yet God has blessed, just up to the measure of the faith and the zeal of His people. It is not for them to be content with this as a sign of His approval, but rather to say, If He has thus blessed our feeble efforts and prayers, what will He not do if we yield ourselves wholly to a life of intercession?

(5) What a call to penitence and confession that our lack of consecration has kept back God's blessing from the world! He was ready to save men, but we were not willing for the sacrifice of a wholehearted devotion to Christ and His service.

Children of God, God counts upon you to take your place before His throne as intercessors. Awake, I pray you, to the consciousness of your holy calling as a royal priesthood. Begin to live a new life in the assurance that intercession, in both the likeness to and the fellowship with the interceding Lord Jesus in heaven, is the highest privilege a man can desire. In this spirit take up the word with large expectations: "Call unto Me, and I will answer thee, and show thee great and mighty things which thou knowest not."

Let each one who has read thus far say whether he is not willing, whether he does not long to give himself wholly to this blessed calling and in the power of Jesus Christ to make intercession, supplication for God's church and people and for a dying world, the one chief object of his life? Is this asking too much? Is it too much to yield your life for this holy service of the royal priesthood to that blessed Lord who gave Himself for us?

Day 31

Intercession, a Divine Reality

*And another angel came...and there was given
unto him much incense, that he should offer it
with the prayers of all saints upon the golden
altar which was before the throne.*
—Revelation 8:3

*A*re the thoughts to which this little book
has given utterance not a sufficiently
grave indictment of the subordinate
place given to intercession in the teaching and
practice of the church with its ministers and
members? Is it not in very deed of such supreme importance as to make it an essential,
altogether indispensable element in the true
Christian life? To those who take God's Word
in its full meaning, there can be no doubt about
the answer. Intercession is, by amazing grace,
an essential element in God's redeeming purpose—so much so that without it the failure of
its accomplishment may lie at our door.

Christ's intercession in heaven is essential to His carrying out of the work He began

upon earth, but He calls for the intercession of the saints in the attainment of His object. Just think of what we read: "And all things are of God, who hath reconciled us to Himself by Jesus Christ, and hath given to us the ministry of reconciliation" (2 Cor. 5:18). As the reconciliation was dependent on Christ's doing His part, so in the accomplishment of the work He calls on the church to do her part. We see how Paul regarded intercession day and night as indispensable to the fulfillment of the work that had been entrusted to him. It is but one aspect of that mighty power of God which works in the heart of His believing people.

Intercession is indeed a divine reality. Without it the church loses one of its chief beauties and loses the joy and the power of the Spirit life for achieving great things for God. Without it, the command to preach the gospel to every creature can never be carried out. Without it, there is no power for the church to recover from her sickly, feeble life and conquer the world. And in the life of the believer, minister, or member, there can be no entrance into the abundant life and joy of daily fellowship with God, except as he takes his place among God's elect—the watchmen and remembrancers of God, who cry to Him day and night. Church of Christ, awake, awake! Listen to the call, "Pray without ceasing" (1 Thess. 5:17). Take no rest, and give God no rest. Let the answer be, even though it be with a sigh from the depths of the heart, "For Zion's sake will I not hold my peace" (Isa. 62:1). God's Spirit will reveal to us the power of a life of intercession as a divine reality, an essential and indispensable element of the great redemption and therefore also of the true Christian life.

May God help us to know and to fulfill our calling!